AF334819

Helen Hooven Santmyer

. . . And Ladies of the Club

Willa Cather

Agatha Christie

Jane Austen

Eudora Welty

for Marianna

A CERTAIN X

Linda Orr

L'Epervier Press

ACKNOWLEDGMENTS

Some of these poems appeared in the following magazines: *Antaeus, Creel, Field, New Rivers, Shenandoah, Specialia, The Yale Lit.*

Library of Congress Cataloging in Publication Data
Orr, Linda, 1943-
A certain x.
I. Title.
PS3565.R724C4 811'.54 80-21424
ISBN 0-934332-24-x

Cover photograph by Lynn Mueller
Book design by Bridget Culligan
Typesetting by Maggie Howell, Portland, Oregon
Printing by Commercial Printing Company,
Fort Collins, Colorado

Special thanks to Bob and Karen Herz and Bill Burtis, without whom I would have been discouraged. And, for their support of this manuscript, to Gaylen Ross, Cathy Iino, Susan Lurie, and David and Elvira Venables.

A CERTAIN X is distributed by Small Press Distribution, 1784 Shattuck Avenue, Berkeley, California 94709.

L'EPERVIER PRESS
Colorado • Washington

CONTENTS

1

AFTER "AFTERWARDS,"
A POEM BY THOMAS HARDY 3
CARS AFTER THE RAIN 5
OF A COUPLE 6
TWO SOUTHERN HOUSES 7
THE CAVING SIDES 9
THE MAN IN PLACE 10
NO EXIT 14
GARRET 15
RED HAT IN SNOW 17
THE LAMP OVER MY RIGHT SHOULDER 18

2

THE GUILLOTINE 21
YOURSELF 25
WHEN I SET OUT 27
CONFESSIONS IN THE
NON-PERSON SINGULAR 28
HERODIAS 30
BUOYANT WORDS 32
BATTERY OF DEFENSES 33

3

FOR SOME 39
FRIENDS WITHOUT WORDS 40
HER VISITS 42
THE BOAT 44
RIVERS INTO RIVERS, NO SEA 45
SOMETIMES YOU WANT THE LONELY LIFE 46
HOW WINTER COMES IN A SENTENCE 47
THREE LITTLE DIRGES 48
DELICATE MEASURE 49
THE QUIETEST PART 50
THE SEQUEL HE TELLS 52
A CERTAIN X 55
NEVER TITLED 56

At nightfall, ardent with music and the speech of friends,
Knowing, through all that harbored time, the light was lessening.

—"The Hourglass"
Weldon Kees

1

AFTER "AFTERWARDS,"
A POEM BY THOMAS HARDY

When minutes shall not mean much, the slim
marks of a day, when I shall have slipped out
as of a pocket, a package someone carries
still embracing the bulk but a gift having
slipped out, never to be shelved and given
again, will my friends say "she was
a tenacious woman with nothing to hold to?"

If, on a late afternoon in fall, wild flowers drop
from plants that start to look alike,
and trees are discernible only in bark
which too is scaling, if then
I expect to be remembered, is it by name
or by the face I never saw myself making
in anger or desire, and will the one
remembering attach any meaning
to my not being there?

Or, milling in a group lumped together in front
of a toystore window, reading the windy
temperature on the mall, the Fair Haven
Bus leaving, someone running for a stray
child, another lifting a heel to examine its wear,
feeding the birds, or rubbing his hands
in the cold, will they all
close in, as if the next in line had just
passed through the door?

Will strangers stop when carlights burn at noon,
craning to look at the casket, at least locate
its bulk inside the car, the survivors
all withdrawn behind their veils,
and into their thoughts,
or will there be survivors, will I
outlive the town elders,
till they muse on Biblical Times,
how years were counted differently then,
but didn't amount to more?

CARS AFTER THE RAIN

Cars pass on a wet street
and the sound is more like itself

than the sound of cars on a street
as if something else moves in

with a storm, unseen, no part
of shadow and black cloud, no part

of clearing either, a change
the twosomes in their coupes will not

notice nor the foursomes, not even
one bundled alone in a coat

watching ahead for the light
to change, he will not notice,

and though I watched the sky striate
with marks of coming rain,

though I saw an actual flash of light,
it did not define the sensation

of more than a minute: the hours
of passing cars like the wash

long after a ship passes hardly
remembered or pointed out as when

your presence started muting its work
on everything I am.

OF A COUPLE

for C.P.

They could keep going
well enough left alone
having honed an intricate
timing of torture
the slow burn of a light
in the eye, the pitch
of something gone wrong gone
unnoticed like hair as far
as it grows, teeth reverting
to the original bite,
they can't go back
but speed up
with nothing ahead
or pushing behind
but one self-portrait after
the next – a collar,
a crushed hat and frizzled
hair lengthen, shrink;
brows arch, knit,
and lower – her face
clears and clouds
as she lies in bed
till the years issue
a funnel of perfume
she presses to her wrist
and the back of his neck
as they rise of themselves
in the scent of the over-
extinct, ash rising
as no flower ever, as trout
open for the torn bread.
The Whirling Death
is a disease fish get,
they spin before floating up,
their mouths parted like lovers'.

TWO SOUTHERN HOUSES

1

The one house I never wanted to see,
that would have shamed me to look upon,
where it used to stand among wisteria and oak
before it too came down, this was the house
I saw when lifting the frame from the closed
blossoms of newspaper print my father had packed.
I knew it was a copy of that house

by the balcony and porch I had glimpsed once,
despite myself: the same picture
among minuature golfers displayed in a den.
My oldest aunt rose up through a trellis
of sun and shook my hand.
How did this hand weave back
to slaves in and out of our tree?

It took me years to ask
what father knew of the only slave
left in the house laying a fire at dawn,
but since I consented to know, this picture
hangs on my wall, a wide front porch,
a balcony as long as the porch sketched
behind a touch of tree and pale green

summer when he himself must have been swimming
nearby in the black river. I picture his body,
I picture the dripping black bodies in summer
horsing around, a far cry from the windows
doubled in glass and framed, yet something
unbroken edges through father's impeccable
style of packing with paper-twisted magnolia.

2

The house in Charlotte my parents built
still stands; you see it rounding the bend
at Ferncliff Road, the in-set door lit,
a ribbon on the mock '90's lamp post also lit,
the backyard aglow, if any flower is out,
especially osmanthus, you take the immediate tour
with pauses to breathe in the air, no other
children but me, the heat blowing upstairs,
the beds made, my parents have another

life but this is the one I see:
father and Richard balanced on either side
of a ladder, laughing while they prune the row
of laurel that separates us from the Ryders.
Father's way of easing laughter,
Richard stretching a tale, black
and white with enough grey for what is left
unsaid. Mother is the one
who has changed: her livingroom, untouched,

the den just so yet she speaks
of the nursing home with more than
her usual concern. Father studies the fire
while she reads the *News.*
Soon they retire to bed and I move upstairs
where I lie awake thinking
they are moored to their needs, both
accepting and not, my will to be suspended
for a while, maybe forever, if I have to.

THE CAVING SIDES

Obsessed with moving, I don't know how
I got here. Sliding backwards
snagging nothing that measures the buckets
of sand? Children growing used to give
the illusion of drawing close to shore:
friends came clear with age, arrival
was a loud thump of rope, a motor shifting
down, yet no one loitered for long.

If only it were not the awkward moments
I remembered best or the words of others
snapped up to fit my needs. Turning them,
I always find the anagrams of my name,
the puns on whore and grammar.
If only I could see what happens between
the frozen pictures, what was squeezed
from the album of childhood, my other
parents. How can I trust
my hallucinations when she sits calmly
in her favorite chair, he raises
a cordial frappé to his smiling lips?
Yes, they *are* in cahoots, and with me.

A thief always precedes the opening
ceremony of the tomb and savory thoughts
from old books chip and soil the white
cotton gloves. I still want work with my hands,
something more or less like words.
On a camping trip I preferred to dig
the latrine; I leaned
over the earth as it opened and the sides
kept caving in, the mad race
against the caving sides, like an overcast
sky pulling forever into itself
on a day neither rain nor sun consumes.

THE MAN IN PLACE

1. *Undefined and Defined*

The man on a limb
has no moon-backing,
a hand projecting shadows

on a dark wall:
the alligator's maw, for instance,
sends a hen flapping over nothing.

A man becoming landscape
absorbs all woodwind
without losing his breath.
Nothing eats at his teeth.

Keeping his weather to himself,
he opens an umbrella in his house,
covers his head,
and reappears in window after window.

2. *The Contrast*

In a roomful of people
he accepts the stillness of chairs.
His rare word is a rest in music.

Leaning over an old man from behind,
he listens: a mountain giving
the plumblossom tree attention.

The dry ice of conversation
moistens windows.
Staring into someone's face,
they would only be talking

to themselves again,
but when he joins them,
they begin to hear a voice
alongside their own.

They begin to listen.
The air clears.
Like a plane in a pocket,
they drop from long nightmares.

3. *Carefully Looking In*

Yet he will descend no further
than six months and a lost friend.
Insight has its own speedlimit,
like tunnels, towns.

His lips stretch to fit a flashlight.
Inside his flickering skull,
a woman scrubs cave paintings
revealing defenses

and hunts of the mind.
His heart is a trap
he won't touch
preferring to work with his hands.

4. *Balance*

In summer, sheets drape
the sofas when he's gone
or the garden, left netted
with a fine spray of whispers.

In return, winter insects
work in his mind.
Full leaf shapes wait,
uninvented, to be chewed.

Outside, the drifts are sabers
and don't soften
the long-leaf pine.
Nothing mounts his steps, but snow.

His kitchen is warm.
Can he stop bottles
from sliding off the table?
After the evening meal,

he draws in deeply
to make a place for no one,
tips his chair back against the wall
while every board and bone settles in.

NO EXIT

1

Here in a small town in Pennsylvania
my "moving" dream found me again and began
the fresh invasion of my doorless room.
Last night I called too long a distance

to hear a friend's gentle reminder
that I am no longer there. In New Haven,
I am afraid I will be my only variety.
In New York I would never sleep.

This week I thought No One had taken over
but I found myself last night
gliding around the rink
and this morning my homeless dream, home.

2

Numbers barely visible on unfamiliar doors,
"no outlet" signs, where you would expect
"no exit" and still no path from one hill
to another without going through the hollow.

This time of year the golden trees are ambiguous
and all desire. They flake and peel
to bark. I may have lost my grandmother's
bracelet in the move. And when my parents die,

I will keep referring back to a point that stays
empty, as if the loss of leaves
will piece the houses across the ledge in,
and discoveries will not be so slow coming out the same.

GARRET

Six flights of stairs with no lift or wings.
Each landing gives me time to think,

which I don't need. Each landing
has its unforeseen disadvantage.

Do boiling turnips irritate the nose?
The woman and her sweatered dog pass.

A man stands aside, anemones in his hand.
Half-way: the rug looks cleaner;

you catch your breath, alarming fewer people.
The wax beans inside my sack grow pale;

my cake has lost its rum.
Here all turns to stone.

A tremendous storm would be the answer!
—In which everyone you knew was killed.

I don't suppose she's talking
to me through that wall.

I'll move on: the coast is clear,
don't need a sea to say that, nor

an ear pressed against my skull.
There's no connection

between that breathing and me.
Here's the last floor.

This is where I lived.
Dust fell all day from my cloth.

Come in.
I'll throw open a window, big as a door.

RED HAT IN SNOW

Past lunch hour though too cold
to press an apple to the teeth
or pour with a gloved hand,

can't do much but walk and that,
difficult, thinking how fragile
the old are, everyone slowing down.

The sidewalk shoveled: winter's
negative harvest over for the moment
where others go and come without

the trace walking in forest leaves
though nothing stands out there either—
lustered flow, off-white

except for cracks of trees in sky.
Stepping like on the moon,
he probably does not want to be alone

if he waves to her watching
from the hill and though on his way
he turns for her scrambling thought

tossed out: ". . . lose yourself
in that red hat?" Too far for words
to carry even after

a slight delay covered over
by a laugh unheard but mimed
as they part and the hat goes on

to dot the slope with brightness
unlike the sun changing in shades
of pink and rose at the day's end.

THE LAMP OVER MY RIGHT SHOULDER

Nothing rustles. The walls have shifted
their allegiance inside to the lamp
over my right shoulder. It is not yet
bizarre to be rich with solitude and I am not yet
a miser in the brothel of my grotesques.

Should I be less quick with bliss, waiting
till I am a hundred and sure it is worth it?
But think: if sitting here has not turned sour,
there is a chance a fire gives warmth without decay
and the body's decline speeding up before my eyes

is more than resigned splendor.
It is hard not to feed off another's loss,
and I almost forgot none of this is mine:
a Normandy farm, my chair, these andirons.
If World War II were not so far back,

I might be a familiar scene: alone at night,
listening closely to the radio's foreign words.
No. I have not forgotten the enemy: why clock
hands are never the same length, why actors and
 the blind
make grand, round gestures, hardly touching
 the furniture.

2

THE GUILLOTINE

for Pierre Albouy (1920-74)

1

all wood but the axe,
runs down niches
through collar to neck,
so there's no slip-up, no jumping
the track of what words do.

Before he finished his novel, *'93,*
Victor Hugo thought he'd be dead
and a lion and thunder.
He gave up mistresses to write,
keeping as many:
"I'll die indignant."

In the shadow of a dolmen,
in the dolmen of Hugo's
bearing, a man pondered
the monumental work
turning prose or poem
into folds of firm skin:

it was rumored he too had a mistress
till taken to bed;
his wife tucked the sheets.
The sheer pages of his "Pléiade"
were too heavy to turn.
Tired, he rested his head.

2

Women grew crazed at the cart's approach;
they tore sheets into shreds (for head bandages or rags)
on church steps watching, or pushed their wares

and fussed with their hair in a twist
or a "guillotine cut" – short at the nape
with a narrow red ribbon around the neck.

Hugo was sure of himself. If anxiety spread
as he let out nothing inside him, chaos around him,
he controlled it with a grasp of madness:

"Titan versus Giant," called God or Language.
He danced like the women where he shouldn't,
on ruins, on graves, on the seaspray dashing high

on Guernsey. In Paris the delicate man read Hugo
with a powerful voice; when his body, effaced in sheets,
became sprigs of bone, the voice didn't fit:

They laid him out on a plank,
they adjusted his neck.
The executioner loosened
his hair out from under.

3

Law decreed the guillotine
should be seen over every head,
3 meters at least.
C'était dressé, plutôt que bâti

(It rose up, was not built.)
Beside the plank two baskets
were ready, one long,
one short and square.

Up early, Hugo wrote
at the mantelpiece, his orange
peelings still pungent, his hands
moved in the trance

of clipping phrases in sections
of orange that almost taste,
almost touch but for mystery
palpable in other ways.

There it was, the hieroglyphic
book, the alphabetic enigma,
the guillotine as a capital *H*
or a *V* crashing onto an *O*.

4

The window is fixed as an *H:*
it stays, the moment, won't mar a winter night
I bathe my head in. Each day my friend
looks out of his own death, pretending not
to see the decline of his face, nor mine.
I too pretend he focuses farther
beyond my visit, beyond his wife's chatter
of how he feels in the third person,
beyond care and cynicism, past his own dimming
voice and Hugo who held onto his ladder
in limbo, his H***, held on 15 years longer
than expected at the end of the novel *Ninety-Three:*
The spring was released; the blade slid, sticking
at first. I thought I had time to watch it
descend as snow moves over mountains No one told me
it happens so fast The blindfold slips a little
for children They see out and cheat
like Hugo turning his tables a waiter
balancing a silver tray toward the man
rising to meet its fall.

YOURSELF

Besides walking through rooms
or down the street, crossing the field
on a seasonal path, besides the passing
fancy, you change form. Nothing anyone
can see who focuses on the cheeks
where a mother's food shows up, or under
the eyes where sleep is supposed to lodge.
They notice a new coat. But this shape
is not related *per se* to the body
the sun throws across the floor, nor is it
the after-effect of a mood: manic or depressed.
You might say it cannot be seen
in terms of change.

Sometimes you're so light
no shadow can find a footing, no wind
a place to spin around, no storm, a niche
for its evil eye, you are what is and nothing
more, you move in one fell swoop whether up
or out. A stream will burrow in, a bird
zero down over the sea but you never think
of comparing yourself to a bird or stream,
for there is no desire to be other
than what comes, beyond the shore, at most
a hum or sigh. Then, almost imperceptibly,
maybe at the same time as feeling one way,
you become someone else.

Not because of a step
taken in time, not from shifting
paces, you accept, to begin with,
the smallest leaf landing in the palm
of your hand, saying this is my self
in reverse, it will see me through.
And that is the sign for all the rest
of the clothes to pile on, now that

you're alone and scared, "wings"
they call the addition on a house
that won't fly, lost in the maze of amaze-
ment, the garden choked with growth.

WHEN I SET OUT

When I set out that night,
        I was determined to change
        or have my life changed
for me by friends who planned
the meeting on a winter night
        in January.

When I set out that night,
        more hopeful than I
        had been in many years,
I wondered even as I went
if meetings only come to pass
        in memory.

When I set out that January night,
        as if being led
        by what I had already lived,
the feeling grew: how it would end,
sooner or later, the way it had begun
        before setting out.

CONFESSIONS IN THE NON-PERSON SINGULAR

Studied because of the others,
dressed like them, weighed
the words that were said,
tried to speak as if
my listener spoke to himself.
Walked with my cage firm,
alert, especially the horror
of complaining and sent
cards home from camp, learned
to swim, before it all broke.
But then did not revert back,
for that would only be more of the same.

Did not sit mystic and still
in the middle of a white-washed
room as a child playing
but without toys.
No, did not remain cut-off
from the rest, deaf and dumb
when it was clear
had only been given a used
beauty to work with, smoke
rising beside the old camera
that shook with anger: no one
under the velvet cloth, no
picture of who looks on.

Even at this late stage
did not refuse food nor the signs
of affection though too late
to strike out on one's own
with a reversible coat

in ribbons: corsage-pink.
No wonder as rain
approaches over the hills,
it is not I who stand like some
to face the storm
but turn my back, a bow-legged
dancer, omega, waiting to be called.

HERODIAS

The breasts seed
and swallow their own seed,
seeding again though no
lips alight and drink,
these blossoms never fall
as if they are painted on
so the girl will not die
when she looks out of the window
into snow. Rouge
from a little pot, the sun
smoothed over the cheeks,
hair liquid twisted
in a comb, a pencil
dipped in the pupil's
well of indelible ink.

Lying on her side,
the left-hand posed
odalisque-like
on the raised left knee
she might feel something or
she might not, it doesn't seem
to matter to the body
that rises now and walks
to the mirror, the hickory
dresser in the back, purple
curtains, half a bed, an ironing
board with a skirt draped
as over a stone.
                                        She is not moved
as others, does not participate
in the same way by giving up
her absence to someone else,
deserting herself, yet she is

not spirit, surely not a soul,
for she does not believe souls
feel this pleasure, equally
erotic, of solitude.

BUOYANT WORDS

Fingers hold on
like trinkets never dusted off
and cows drift in from the daily
munching to be milked
as if they could go on forever,
as if the wind were sweet

and could whistle: I'm not
an herb whose odor is unctuous
when cut, I feel waiting
running out, the end
of knowledge and mending.
Rabbits, caterpillars

strew irreparable leaves.
At least I'm not pessimistic,
giving in to the caravans
of Gypsies, the pastry
peddler at my door.
I take to sweeping, not weeping.

Joy! Eternity! Buoyant words
still make me sit up and sing.
But yesterday I stood an hour
watching the setting sun not come out.
And this morning was a fog
and at noon the stores closed.

BATTERY OF DEFENSES

1

No, three showers a day do not make you
compulsive, it's American,
yet you still sit alone at the bar.

A web of nerves in your cheek catches
the slightest notion of trouble,
and, though you keep your distance,

it is all around.
Facing each other over wooden tables,
a man and woman in every booth

don't hear their voices rise
as each tries to force back the someone absent
he can't, she can't get to.

3

What you're not telling me does not matter:
I've imagined it.
You come into my life wearing your room

that swells or collapses like an oxygen tent,
the room that moves out
over risky fields at night,

over other couples who have willed
passion on themselves
as medicine for all their mistakes.

Your room meets me sleeping
in my room that is sleepwalking
with its doors open.

2

You prefer fishers of fish,
a few hairs curling around the collar
as their old t-shirts,

their minds wandering no farther
than a round of drinks.
I have noticed that you never eat

when drinking for months,
that the crude fool has a clean body,
that the punctuation *fuckin*

before each word is the whistle
of a man with a trach
who plugs holes each time he speaks.

3

FOR SOME,

Slipping away is easy.
Secrets won't keep them,
the hush building a plot.
They sense the unguarded door
when the car arrives. No one
has to show them out; they go
without cries and horns.
If they want to be alone
for long periods of time,
it is not arrogance nor
as easy as it seems.

Even those who like deserted
streets and landscapes
are realistic, answering
a personal call
to step into the next room
where someone is ready for bed.
They have to make the most
of excuses, easing out
of ties with others
at moments of relative
calm and honesty.

They are never above
a joke, though don't expect
the tension to end.
Solitude is their sole
dependent but they wonder
if this self-sufficiency
isn't a trick against them.
A lull in the conversation
and they turn aside
with a simple reason for leaving,
implying how serious it is.

FRIENDS WITHOUT WORDS

for Mary Swander

I linger
making backward swimming motions
into my coat; you rush up
with something in your hand:
a comb, a pack of cough drops
from my chair: "So I did."
We walk downstairs to the door
I hold after passing till you
catch it. The least you can do
is a question: "Just wondering
if I need this heavy coat."

We begin by talking,
mistake the ear for the heart.
After months of sitting up,
killing night after night,
your mother does not die,
but I know your family's flaw
and you know what I would have
changed. Nor am I the same
person who stood that morning
at the top of the stairs,
precarious, yet stable
enough to be friends.

Now we dismiss the small talk
quickly and find most talk
small though how else were we
to begin? Our rest
does not come from nowhere

though it seems to: arms
looped around each other's
neck not really tired
our heads close in,
we're ear to ear,
pure listen.

HER VISITS
for Wallace Fowlie

When my younger sister
came back from France
the first time she had clothes
and perfume that swept the house
as if she had come upon
a stolen treasure all at once.

Her face was a movie
star's, the thin line
of her eyebrows traced the delicate
script of Europe,
unreadable to us.

She could no longer find words
for common things
and uncommon emotions,
she maintained, were best left
in the original.

So she set her phrases
to a music whose sense
both escaped and filled us.

The neighbors would not sit
next to her on the sofa
out of a new deference: before,
they hoped she would pass through
her stages entering at last
one of theirs.

Now she has gone
into a face she keeps up
on our walks together
speaking of her husband
and children, the Portuguese
maid but never of mother
and father who are also
gone, of their last
harmless words.

Her ability to explain
the most basic needs
is now seriously impaired,
and though I have picked up some
French myself, soon
she won't come back.
Soon she'll stay in Paris
for oysters on New Year's Eve
or rabbit stew in the fall.

Soon she'll travel only
to Normandy which is better, perhaps,
for both of us, since neither she
nor I can bear the strain
of her wanting to come home
somewhere again.

THE BOAT

for Elizabeth Libbey

Rain cannot always blow in
as far as you are standing,
nor has it ruined every grave.
Somewhere wood is sound
and water swells between the same
troughs under any wind, under one
boat that does not turn
as the weight shifts.
Still, an exchange between hands
seems tentative and one person
is the preparation for another.

If somewhere a bridge is out, so what?
It is not there to cross over
when you need it; it is not there
when you fall and spin.
It cannot stop the feelings of fading
in late afternoon; it cannot stop
the weakness of clothes,
nor the lowering of a voice
to patch up silence.

Yet something is not implied
in the turning and chewing.
Something stays seated, when the land slides.

RIVERS INTO RIVERS, NO SEA

I was a girl dangling
my feet in a stream's meandering
noose. I ate too much from the dead
who fed me there by deposit.
The black oval of the oak tree,
its soft mirror, might have been
my car's target, but I left home
before it happened.

I would not let fish follow
nor quail. I had to catch up:
toss walls and trees into the air
to find out what would fit
when I got my figure back.
Not much did. Now a hall
has been home long enough,
but the doors I would enter
are dominoes, not doors.

People are playing leapfrog
over graves. Children grab
for keeps. Grown-ups keep away.
Nothing's livable.
I pick at my food with pins,
in the careless wind a flame dies,
I revert to the instinct of stars,
going when I'm rowed.

SOMETIMES YOU WANT THE LONELY LIFE

Sometimes you want the lonely life
back again, the few friends you would call
on sleepless nights, the magic link
between insomniacs, some famous like Bergman
who listens to country music by his bedroll
on the island, these comforts make you
almost content with your complaints. Or the record
of Wallace Stevens reading his poems, an oracular fatigue
lowers you into sleep as if a large man
stood in the doorway radiating cold
like love. Whatever noise awakens you
is never one you hear but gather yourself up
while traffic grows in the street and the sun
slumps over the sill. In the light of day
the brute parts of yourself snagged and lashing
in the imagined wind lose their glee for the "inner
pocket novel" and you look out of place
standing before your mirror in all these socks
and sweaters like an Eskimo dressed for the encounter
with ten caribou and the god of lemmings.

HOW WINTER COMES IN A SENTENCE

I don't mind that birds leave
in mid-conversation,
that the level of field
drops three feet overnight

and crops flood the market
about the same time my cold toes
seem to disappear
back up my feet like the fingers

of gloves emptied too fast of their inhabitants
as before any disaster
when some cocklebur
of an old woman can't bear to part with

her home even if it means
holding onto the last chimney
after everything else has gone
underground: rather, it's her defiance

that disarms me or why the red berries
of a certain shrubbery (not holly)
don't follow their rightful leaves down,
why they cling to discomfort

beside the dried hydrangea
blooming brown and heavy
on stripped stems
as the dirt closes for winter.

THREE LITTLE DIRGES

1

If the lights go out, light a candle.
If the candle melts, strike a match.
If the match doesn't last, get sticks moving.
If the sticks are wet, stay in bed.

2

How strange to see death surround
you like a rain storm
blurring grandparents first
then the last screen, parents,
and in odd sequence
from the beginning, friends
are going: the fan widens
at the hottest part of the day,
flies amass, you kick the dry clay
under your swing and push.

3

It's logical death should follow us
around like this, the coffin's crony,
my morning shower: a normal day has too many
dresses, and night is only provisional

cover since no one can hoard
sleep like pewter and maize you might
be able to use in packing a sepulchre.
But nothing is heavier than the eyelids'

fall and flicker on last-minute memories
breaking their years of silence.
The towel in the guestroom is purely aesthetic
or over his arm when he serves the drop.

DELICATE MEASURE

I think about the worries
I have now, small and insignificant,
that I bear with little heart, and I think
about multiplying that until I can bear
no more: how much would it take?
I hardly know the extent of damage
to my mother's body, much less
my own; though she travels and sails
with reluctance, still she travels and sails.
The most you can say is: we will change
or we won't. But what if we don't?
Then you blame a lack of will,
asking for patience till the choice
is clear. And if it never is?
Despite a stiff breeze, a tempest
or two, time drifting toward the grave,
what if choices stay perfectly matched?
When a new feather is added, yes,
so a quill, plucked from the most
graceful of felt hats, a white egret,
or a warrior's crown, a feather
used in the signing of the last will
and testament, is also added: no.

THE QUIETEST PART

I could delay his death
until tomorrow night but it's dawn
and I've only fifty more pages to read, an hour's
worth at my hurried pace and the sun's,
before the spell of this long evening's wealth
will end. I keep looking out the window
to check the progress of the light, looking back
at my book and reading as fast as I can
while the birds build their song and the room
begins to glow an imperceptible pearl.
Soon the day nurse will arrive and lift
the shades. I hold onto my book until I am
sure he has died as the sun rises and the book
he is reading in the book slides from his hands
I cannot hold. There is no crash.
The sun is the quietest part of dawn,
a red body finally pulling itself
from behind a stretch of land that makes a path
for the rest of the day, a steady climb
and fall. All night, I watched a man's life
miss its height and keep going as if nothing
had happened nor would. He was the happiest
when his daughter sat beside him in the room
where he worked with a strange, blind force.
Nothing turned out as he planned. But he did not know
the emotion of those hours till later
when they were lost. The night he knew, it snowed.
Then he was as close to himself and the objects
in his room, even his absent daughter.
That was not what he wanted but what he realized
was. The sun has now come out and shines
on a man going for an early walk. He doesn't
even turn or look to his feet. He doesn't appear

the least bit alarmed. Walls we cease to worry about
wash over. The curtain swings back in front
of my face when I let it slip, though
for all I know, the birds and walker stay on.

THE SEQUEL HE TELLS

for Alexandre Aspel

1

I try to follow. Yes, once
I dreamed about a bomb.
I ran home from school too late
to catch my parents.
The streets were still.

He left with them – Paris, 1940–
on foot or in carts,
piled high with a mattress or two,
like whales dragged inland.
He left and was left by
more barges of men than could be saved.

The parades I'm used to
break and mend themselves
a thousand times
over the exception, the man
pointed out by a bullet.

2

As a child he filed by schooltables
where corpses thawed
while the Russian earth
digested last year's.
The soldiers Red or White were one giant
stepping through town.

For me bodies are always wakable.
Sometimes I want them to stay down
when they fall. I want to touch
or watch somebody dead. I resented
the stranger in a stained shirt
who stood up, unmurdered, and took his gun.

Even the men in my own family
betray me: they wander off
like our dogs
the day before their deaths
to the place they plan
to lie down in.

3

In Paris, down the street from the daily
shootings, he finally learned to sleep
six hours. He got up, dressed
and biked to work on the day
his closest friend wasn't there
to meet him for coffee.

His face wavered
for only a minute in the steam
of the cup he held.
The wind never got the smell out
between buildings. Here the Mississippi
is the wind's runway:
you'd think it would lift him

as small now as then, his white hair,
fuller than his shoulders.
In good weather he walks across the bridge
for coffee and unsalted fries.
He apologizes for giving me dreams
that still might come true.

A CERTAIN X

I write to those I used to speak to,
speak to those I wrote to.
For each nothing is lacking: my story
stands on its own though
innuendoes are the wake of any motion.
As long as I talk like them,
mouth their mistakes, they forget
I have a past and mystery

gives way to my own napkin.
A room is no consolation for change.
Walls closing keep the same dimensions:
death might as well be anywhere,
for something looms before the lingering goes,
some violent or bright contrast
makes analogy die, nostalgia—
nothing travels in time.

A curtain of senses descends on any bed:
someone walking stairs unseen,
cabinet doors open at dusk in the grey
play of angles, a squint of sun.
The shelves remodel their jars,
and I adjust my falling body,
extending my notion of youth.
The "dark side" is a myth to keep me here

when I would be everywhere separately,
and my perspective is a child that was air
whistling from a wet bottle cap
or the Tunisian flute from down the hall.
Something looms before the lingering's gone.
The present has to grow out of proportion,
my retinue be the joy
of a thousand X's, their uniqueness.

NEVER TITLED

Names don't help
separate people out
if a town generalizes
to dust or a polliwog
exists. Nothing specific
looking into the future
always walking
down a hall that turns
and bends with no house
or street: no crow
describing passage.

If someone else's name
is the food and music
you evolve through,
a hurricane is life,
like wind but faster
and that, relative.
I haven't felt a feeling
that wasn't a wheel.
Or been in a room
that didn't slant.
Sometimes the story
starts over on the back
and you don't bother
to link syllables up
but get the gist,
recalling the cover,
approximately where
it was on the shelf.